THE ROAD TO SPIRITUAL FITNESS

THE *ROAD* TO *SPIRITUAL FITNESS*

DANNY ABRAMOWICZ

SOPHIA INSTITUTE PRESS
Manchester, New Hampshire

Sophia Institute Press
Box 5284, Manchester, NH 03108
1-800-888-9344

www.SophiaInstitute.com

Sophia Institute Press® is a registered trademark of Sophia Institute.

Names: Abramowicz, Danny, author.
Title: The road to spiritual fitness : a five-step plan for men / Danny
   Abramowicz.
Description: Manchester, New Hampshire : Sophia Institute Press, 2019. |
   Includes bibliographical references. | Summary: "Outlines practical
   steps for Catholic men to strive to live holy lives"— Provided by
   publisher.
Identifiers: LCCN 2019040024 | ISBN 9781644130957 | ISBN
9781644130964
   (epub)
Subjects: LCSH: Catholic men—Religious life.
Classification: LCC BX2352.5 .A268 2019 | DDC 248.8/42—dc23
LC record available at https://lccn.loc.gov/2019040024

I would like to dedicate this guidebook to the priests and laymen who have influenced me to strive for holiness, by spiritually directing me and challenging me.

Fr. William McCandless, O.S.B.

Fr. Peter Armenio, Opus Dei

Fr. Tom Cronin, S.J.

Fr. Augustine Foley, O.S.B.

Deacon "Buzzy" Giennie

Benny Suhor

THE ROAD TO SPIRITUAL FITNESS

MEN, I DON'T KNOW ABOUT YOU, but I believe with all my heart that Jesus Christ wants us men to start taking our Catholic Faith more seriously. In other words, to become more spiritually fit. St. Paul tells us,

> "Train yourselves in godliness; for while bodily training is of some value, godliness is of value in every way, as it holds promise for the present life and also for the life to come" *(1 Tim. 4:7–8)*.

In these trying times for society and the Church, it behooves us to take a personal inventory of our lives, especially interiorly, to see where we stand in regard to our faith life.

We won't have an enduring impact on this world through a bunch of words; we must each pray individually and ask the Holy Spirit to change our hearts so that we can become holy men of God.

Recent credible surveys indicate that, for every person who enters the Catholic Church, six leave. This is alarming. How do we stop this mass exodus?

I believe that the answer lies in male spirituality. We men must step up to the plate and decide in our hearts whether Jesus Christ and His teachings and His Holy Catholic Church are worth fighting for. This is a time for us to run toward, not away from, Jesus and His Church.

Jesus faced the same situation when many of His disciples walked away from Him. In John 6:67–69,

> "Jesus said to the Twelve, 'Will you also go away?' Simon Peter answered him, 'Lord to whom shall we go? You have the words of eternal life; and we have believed and have come to know, that you are the Holy One of God.' "

When Jesus called a group of ordinary men to follow Him and become His Apostles and disciples (and when, some years later, St. Paul did the same), those men had to ask themselves some important questions before answering the call.

Although over the centuries the Lord has never stopped calling men to become holy men of God, men have been reluctant to answer this call. Yet again today, He is reaching out to us ordinary men and asking us to become His disciples. I firmly believe that, through His Word, He will train us who answer this call to become disciples who will transform our confused world.

Many leaders in our Church, both clergy and laypeople, believe that we are at a crossroads in salvation history. Even though Jesus tells us that He "has overcome the world" (John 16:33), the decisions that we all make concerning our faith will have a dramatic impact on the number of souls who will be lost for all eternity.

So before you decide whether to respond to this call to holiness, reflect on the following to determine whether you are up to this challenge.

Will you:

- » Spend the necessary time in studying the teachings of Jesus Christ and His Church?
- » Be a brave warrior who lives and defends the Faith?
- » Be a loyal follower of the Word of God daily?
- » Be willing to stand up to the challenge that Jesus put before us to become a holy man of God?
- » Boldly evangelize others, especially your family, in the Faith?

- » Be courageous like St. Paul and not hesitate to speak out when faith and morals are under attack?
- » Be a devoted spiritual leader in your family?
- » Dedicate yourself to the Blessed Mother to live a chaste life always?
- » Be a strong defender of religious liberty and the right to life?
- » Be totally open to the power of the Holy Spirit to change your heart so that you can love and serve God and others?

The famous Jesuit priest and author Fr. Jean Pierre de Caussade, in his book *Abandonment to Divine Providence*, eloquently states the importance of holiness in man's life. Divine activity permeates the universe and pervades every creature; wherever they are, it is there. It goes before them, it goes with them, and it follows them. All they have to do is to let the waves envelop them.

Would to God that all men could know how easy it is to arrive at a high degree of sanctity! You have only to fulfill the simple duties of Christianity and your state in life, to embrace with submission the crosses belonging to that state, and to submit with faith and love to the designs of Providence in all those things that have to be done or suffered, without going out of your way to seek such things.

This is the spirit by which the patriarchs and the prophets were animated and sanctified before there were so many systems and so many masters of the spiritual life. This is the spirituality of all ages and of every state. No state of life can, assuredly, be sanctified in a more exalted manner, nor in a more wonderful and easy way than by the simple use of the means that God, the sovereign director of souls, gives us to do or to suffer at each moment.

In other words, we *should let go and let God!*

Our world and our Church desperately need men to rise up now and become "spiritual tough guys" like Jesus, St. Joseph, and St. Paul.

Ask yourself: "If not now, then when? And if not I, then who?"

INSTRUCTIONS
To get the most out of this guide:

■ Take your time! It's a long journey.

■ Meditate and allow the Holy Spirit to speak to your heart.

■ Read each Scripture passage and any related texts.

■ Read, reread, and reflect on each paragraph cited from the ***Catechism of the Catholic Church (CCC)***. One paragraph will send you to another or to Scripture passages that will be very helpful.

■ Underline passages that you feel the Holy Spirit is using to speak to you directly.

■ Start a prayer journal.

■ Finally, feel free to add notes to this guide.

///

ROAD TO SPIRITUAL FITNESS
COURSE OF ACTION

///

THE ROAD TO SPIRITUAL FITNESS

ANSWER THE UNIVERSAL CALL TO HOLINESS

My own call to holiness

THIRTY-FIVE YEARS AGO, when I was at a very low point of my life, the Lord spoke to my heart, telling me that He wanted me to change my life and follow Him and become a holy man of God. My reply from the bottom of my heart was, "Yes, Lord, I do want to change—please help me." Thus began my long spiritual journey toward holiness.

We might not be able to attain perfect holiness on this earth, but I do believe that God wants us all to strive for it with everything we have. The journey is long and can be arduous, with many ups and downs, trials, obstacles and tribulations, but be encouraged: God will be with you every step of the way, through the power of the Holy Spirit.

There were many times along the way when I wanted to turn back, but the Lord was there for me and told me, "I never said it would be easy—I only said it would be worth it."

In the following pages, I will share with you my thirty-five-year journey toward holiness, in hopes that it may be helpful to you in your journey. All the information here is from the teachings of Jesus Christ and His Roman Catholic Church:

none of it is just my opinion! Nor is this a deep, theological, philosophical treatise. It's strictly down to earth: it presents you with the fundamentals of our Catholic Faith and shows you how to live in accordance with them.

Let's begin the journey!

MY REFLECTIONS

_____

_____

_____

_____

_____

_____

_____

_____

_____

_____

Tools for *your* road to holiness

What I relate to you in these pages, I learned from the following, which I think will be helpful to you, too:

» The Word of God (the Bible). I recommend the **Didache Bible (RSV Catholic edition),** because it has commentaries based on the **Catechism**

» The teachings of the Church as found in the **Catechism**

» Various prayers, meditations, and reflections

» Many Marian devotions

» My spiritual journaling

» The lives of the saints and the spiritual writings of lay leaders

» Common sense!

MY REFLECTIONS

_____

_____

_____

_____

_____

_____

_____

_____

WHAT THE *CATECHISM* AND SCRIPTURE SAY ABOUT TEMPTATIONS AND SIN

Paul, in his letter to the Romans (5:20), stated,

> "Where sin increased, grace abounded all the more." God continually makes available all the grace we need to resist temptation and overcome sin. We only need to ask for it in faith. (*see CCC 412*)

> "The whole of man's history has been a story of combat with the powers of evil, stretching, so our Lord tells us, from the very dawn of history until the last day. Finding himself in the midst of the battlefield man has to struggle to do what is right, and it is at great cost to himself, and aided by God's grace, that he succeeds in achieving his own integrity." (*CCC 409, quoting* Gaudium et Spes *37*)

> "I do not understand my own actions. For I do not do what I want, but I do the very thing I hate.... For I know nothing good dwells within me, that is, in my flesh. I can will what is right, but I cannot do it. For I do not do what I want, but the evil I do not want is what I do. Now if I do what I do not want, it is no longer I that do it, but sin which dwells within me.... Wretched man that I am! Who will deliver me from this body of death? Thanks be to God through Jesus Christ our Lord!" (*Rom. 7:15, 18–20, 24–25*)

Put on the armor of God

Paul, in Ephesians 6:10–20, tells us that we must put on the whole armor of God in order to rise victorious in the battle against evil. It is a battle not primarily against human persons, but against demonic spirits, and it must be fought with spiritual weapons given to us by God. These weapons include the truth of the Gospel, the practice of the Faith, meditation on the Word of God, and prayer. Furthermore, it is our task as Christians to imbue every aspect of our lives with prayer. Only in this way can there be a Christianization of this world.

MY REFLECTIONS

Be not afraid

O let not your foot slip, or your eye be false, or your ear dull, or your attention flagging! Be not dispirited; be not afraid; keep a good heart; be bold; draw not back; you will be carried through. Whatever troubles come on you—of mind, body, or estate; from within or from without; from chance or from intent; from friends or foes—whatever your trouble be, though you be lonely, O children of a heavenly Father, be not afraid! Acquit you like men in your day; and when it is over, Christ will receive you to Himself, and your heart shall rejoice, and your joy no man taketh from you. *–J.H. Newman, "Warfare the Condition of Victory"*

MY REFLECTIONS

Arm yourself with four spiritual-combat weapons

In his book *The Spiritual Combat*, Fr. Lawrence Scupoli mentioned the four weapons needed in spiritual combat.

1 **Humility and self-distrust**

The first weapon is humility and self-distrust. By "humility," Scupoli means the virtue by which man attributes to God all the good he possesses, and by "self-distrust," he intends a serious assent to the truth that we are human beings wounded by original sin and liable to do bad things.

2 **Hope and confidence in God**

The second weapon is the practice of the virtue of hope and confidence in God. What we should hope for is eternal happiness, and we should be confident that God will provide us with the means to attain that happiness.

3 **Spiritual exercises**

The third weapon is what he calls spiritual exercise. By this, he means the systematic efforts we undertake to cooperate with God's grace to build up Christian virtues, such as patience and charity, and to root out vices, such as sloth and unchastity.

4 **Prayer**

The fourth weapon is the practice of prayer, which ought to be at the center of our lives. St. Thomas teaches that the end, or goal, of our prayer is to be united with God in love. In prayer, we draw nearer to the Lord, and Christ draws us closer to Himself. It is from the living contact with God through Christ that we find and are given the desire and the strength to go on with the struggle both to gain our sanctification and to make the Lord better known and better loved.

All of us must call on the Holy Spirit and ask for the gift of fortitude. Fortitude, or courage, allows us to rise above temptation, fear, persecution, and other trials as we strive to emulate Christ's life and implement His words. This gift of the Holy Spirit gives us the necessary graces to embrace the cross and profess the Faith amid adversities and obstacles. Part of this fortitude includes the supernatural hope of a reward that surpasses the joys and pleasures of the present life (*see CCC 1808*).

MY REFLECTIONS

DEVELOP A GOOD SPIRITUAL ATTITUDE

True holiness and spirituality do not consist, Fr. Scupoli insists, in "exercises which are pleasing to us and comfortable to our nature," but only in those that "nail that nature with all its works to the cross" and that "by renewing the whole man by the practice of the virtues, unite him to his crucified Savior and Creator." Scupoli says that the spiritual life consists in the following principles:

1. We must come to know about and accept the goodness and greatness of God and of our nothingness and inclination to all evil.
2. We are to love God and hate ourselves.
3. We are to subject ourselves not to Him alone but also, for love of Him, to all His creatures.
4. Our love for God must show itself in our uniting ourselves to Him by trying to do what He wants us to do.
5. Finally, our motive for doing all this must be for the glory of God and because God, being who He is, deserves to be so loved and served.

How do we use these principles in such a way that they will serve as a basis for our spiritual lives and affect our

(*continued*)

DEVELOP A GOOD SPIRITUAL ATTITUDE
(*CONTINUED*)

practice of the Faith? We have to ponder the following truths of our Faith and try to see how they affect us personally.

God created you in His image and likeness. (*see Gen. 1:27; CCC 371, 382*)

God sent His only-begotten Son, Jesus Christ, for the salvation of your soul. (*see John 3:16; CCC 430, 432*)

God sent His Holy Spirit to guide you through this life. (*John 14:26; CCC 243–244*)

God gave you His Blessed Mother as your intercessor. (*John 19:27; CCC 2677, 2679*)

"For I am the LORD your God; consecrate yourselves therefore, and be holy, for I am holy." (*Lev. 11:44*)

"You, therefore, must be perfect, as your heavenly Father is perfect." (*Matt. 5:48*)

"As he who called you is holy, be holy yourselves in all your conduct; since it is written, 'You shall be holy, for I am holy.'" (*1 Pet. 1:15–16*)

"All Christians in any state or walk of life are called to the fullness of Christian life and to the perfection of charity." All are called to holiness. (*CCC 2013;* LG *40*)

"The prime and fundamental vocation that the Father assigns to each of the lay faithful in Jesus Christ through the Holy Spirit: The vocation to holiness that is the perfection of charity. Holiness is the greatest testimony of the dignity conferred on a disciple in Christ." (*John Paul II,* Christifidelis Laici *16*)

"He chose us in him before the foundation of the world, that we should be holy and blameless before him." (*Eph. 1:4*)

"Indeed, having shown that the Spirit is the source and giver of all holiness, we now confess that it is he who has endowed the Church with holiness." The Church is, in a phrase used by the Fathers, the place "where the Spirit flourishes." (*CCC 749, quoting* Roman Catechism *I, 10, 1 and St. Hippolytus,* Trad. Ap. *35: S Ch 11, 118*)

(*continued*)

DEVELOP A GOOD SPIRITUAL ATTITUDE
(*CONTINUED*)

> We must prepare for a trial and battle: "By virtue of their kingly mission, lay people have the power to uproot the rule of sin within themselves and in the world, by their self-denial and holiness of life." (*CCC 943; cf. LG 36*)

> The way of perfection passes by way of the Cross. There is no holiness without renunciation and spiritual battle. (*CCC 2015; cf. 2 Tim. 4*)

Cultivate a rich spiritual life

Jesus tell us in Matthew 5:48, "You, therefore, must be perfect as your heavenly Father is perfect." Striving for perfection and holiness is the way we become united with God, and being united with God gives sense and purpose to our life.

The notion of becoming holy does not sit well with Catholic men. Whether this is because we tend to distrust claims about human holiness or because we have been taught to accept ourselves as we are, holiness to many people seems to be an unreal or even empty concept when applied to human beings.

It is easy to have vague ideas what perfection is, which serve well enough to talk about, when we do not intend to aim at it; but as soon as a person really desires and sets about seeking it himself, he is dissatisfied with anything but what is tangible and clear, and constitutes some sort of direction towards the practice of it. –*J.H. Newman, "A Short Road to Perfection"*

MY REFLECTIONS

Seek a profound change of heart

"Few souls understand what God would accomplish in them if they were to abandon themselves unreservedly to Him and if they were to allow His grace to mold them accordingly." –*St. Ignatius of Loyola*

Everything that we do either personally or collectively should have as our target goal the changing of hearts. The **Catechism** states it very well in the following two paragraphs.

The heart is the dwelling place where I am, where I live; according to the … Biblical expression, the heart is the place "to which I withdraw." The heart is our hidden center, beyond the grasp of our reason and of others; only the Spirit of God can fathom the human heart and know it fully. The heart is the place of decision, deeper than our psychic drives. It is the place of truth, where we choose life or death. It is the place of encounter, because as an image of God we live in relation: It is the place of covenant. (CCC 2563)

Scripture speaks sometimes of the soul or the spirit, but most often the heart (more than a thousand times). According to scripture it is the heart that prays. If our heart is far from God, the words of prayer are in vain. (CCC 2562)

The following are just three of more than a thousand Scripture passages that speak of the heart:

> I will give them one heart, and put a new spirit within them; I will take the stony heart out of their flesh and give them a heart of flesh, that they may walk in my statutes and keep my ordinances and obey them: and they shall be my people, and I will be their God. *(Ezek. 11:19–20)*

> Jesus said, "You shall love the Lord your God with all your heart, and with all your soul, and with all your mind. This is the great and first commandment." *(Matt. 22:37–38)*

> For where your treasure is, there will your heart be also. *(Matt. 6:21)*

MY REFLECTIONS

Make the most of your time

When a person's life is coherent with his faith, true wisdom is the result; and this immediately leads him to make the most of his time (to redeem time). "Redeeming time," St. Augustine explains, means sacrificing, when the need arises, present interests in favor of eternal ones and purchasing eternity with the coin of time.

The Greek word *kairos* refers to the content of that point in time in which we find ourselves, the situation that it creates, and the opportunities that that very moment offers as regards to the ultimate purpose of this life.

Hence, making the most of our time means much more than not wasting a moment; it means using every situation and every moment to give glory to God.

Time is a treasure that melts away. It escapes from us, slipping through our fingers like water through the mountain rocks. Tomorrow will soon be another yesterday. Our lives are so very short. Yesterday has gone and today is passing by, but what a great deal can be done for the love of God in this short space of time. —*Josemaría Escrivá, Friends of God, no. 52*

TO READ
- Eph. 5:15–17
- Sir. 39:16–17
- Matt. 24:42, 44; 25:13
- Mark 13:32–33
- CCC 672–673

MY REFLECTIONS

_____

_____

_____

_____

_____

_____

_____

_____

_____

_____

_____

_____

_____

_____

_____

_____

_____

RELY ON GOD'S WINNING FORMULA: THE FOUR W'S

ON MY JOURNEY toward holiness, the Lord wanted me first to take inventory of my interior spiritual life. With much prayer, reflection, and meditation on Sacred Scripture, and directed by the power of the Holy Spirit, I was able to design what I call "God's Winning Formula," based on four W's. Here is how to use God's Winning Formula:

» Begin by asking yourself the questions listed below each W. Answer them truthfully, remembering that this is between you and the Lord.

» Reflect on your answers, and then ask the Holy Spirit to direct you to make the necessary choices regarding each W. Making proper choices will help you in your efforts to become a holier man of God.

» Finally, continue to pray and ask the Holy Spirit to give you the strength and courage to stay committed to God's Winning Formula. It's not a program: it's a way of life!

1. The *Will of God* is your conversion

"Not everyone who says to me, 'Lord, Lord,' will
enter the kingdom of heaven, but only the one
who does the will of my Father in heaven."
(*Matt. 7:21, CCC 2822–2827*)

Ask yourself:

» Do I follow the will of God or my will?
» Do I live according to my ways or God's ways?
» Is Jesus Christ my highest priority?
» Do I have a personal relationship with Jesus?
» Do I give God a fair share of my time?
» Do I communicate with God through prayer?

The answers I have given:

» I'm committed to following God's will—not my way
but His way (*see Eph. 5:17; Rom. 12:1–2; James 4:13–15*).
» I've decided to make Jesus the number-one priority in
my life. As St. Augustine says: "Our hearts are restless
until they rest in Thee" (*Confessions 1, 1; see Sir. 15:14–
17; John 6:67–69*).

» I've established a personal relationship with Jesus Christ, making Him the center of my heart *(see Mark 8:27–30; John 15:4–5; CCC 308)*.

» I've made prayer the foundation of my Faith life, grounded in the Holy Spirit *(see 1 Thess. 5:16–19; Eph. 6:18; CCC 2826, 1073)*.

MY REFLECTIONS

2. The *Word of God* is for your transformation

"Indeed, the word of God is living and effective, sharper than any two-edged sword, penetrating even between soul and spirit, joint and marrow, and able to discern reflections and thoughts of the heart" *(Heb. 4:12; see CCC 101–133).*

Ask yourself:

» Do I read and reflect on God's Word in Holy Scripture?

» Do I truly believe that the Holy Spirit is the principal author of Scripture and that He guided and inspired its human authors?

» Do I read and have my family read the Scripture readings before Sunday Mass?

» Do I spend time studying the **Catechism of the Catholic Church**?

The answers I have given:

» I came to realize that the only way to get to know Jesus personally was to read and reflect on His Word *(see 2 Tim. 3:15–17; John 20:30–31).*

» To grow in my Catholic Faith, I use the tools provided to us: the **Bible** (our playbook), the **Catechism** (our game plan) and the teachings of the Church (the **Magisterium**) *(see CCC 85–87; 101ff.; 1 Thess. 2:13; 2 Pet. 1:19–21; John 21:24–25)*.

» I try to become holy because that's what Jesus asks of each of us *(see 1 Pet. 1:15–16; Eph. 1:3–5; CCC 941, 1426)*.

» I prepare for every Mass by reading that day's Scripture readings *(see Luke 24:25–27, 44–45; CCC 135, 137, 141)*.

MY REFLECTIONS

3. Your *Witness for Christ* is evangelization of others

Everyone who acknowledges me before
others I will acknowledge before my heavenly
Father. But whoever denies me before
others, I will deny before my heavenly
Father. *(Matt 10:32–33, CCC 2044–2046)*

Ask yourself:

» Do I witness on behalf of Christ by my words and actions, especially to my family?

» Do I truly believe in the Real Presence of Jesus in the Eucharist?

» Do I live a life based on faith and morals?

» Do I stand up for godly principles?

The answers I have given:

» The best way I can witness for Jesus is in the breaking of the Bread, the Eucharistic Sacrifice of the Mass *(see John 6:51, 53–54; Luke 22:19–20; CCC 1382–1384, 1391–1392)*.

» I've resolved to attend Mass daily, because I know this will transform my life and, I hope, make me a better disciple *(see John 6:33–34, 58).*

» I try to witness to others by boldly proclaiming Jesus Christ through my words but, more importantly, by the way I live my life, day in and day out *(see 1 John 3:18–19; John 15:26–27; Matt. 5:16; James 5:19–20).*

» I strive to ensure that every facet of my life is grounded in godly principles *(Eph. 4:22–24; Col. 3:16–17; James 1:22; CCC 2475).*

MY REFLECTIONS

4. Your *Winning Crown* is eternal salvation

"I have competed well; I have finished the
race; I have kept the faith. From now on the
crown of righteousness awaits me, which
the Lord, the just judge, will award to me
on that day, and not only to me, but to all
who have longed for his appearance" *(2 Tim.
4:7–8, NABRE; CCC 1044–1045, 1050).*

Ask yourself:

» Do I concentrate more on earthly possessions and
recognition than on the crown of eternal salvation?

» Do I look to Jesus as the way, the truth, and the life?

» Do I realize that my salvation comes through Christ,
or do I think I can earn it or buy it? What role does
our Blessed Mother play?

» Do I believe that Christ died for me personally?

The answers I have given:

» I've realized that earthly crowns will never satisfy me;
only God can do so. "For what will it profit a man,
if he gains the whole world and forfeits his life?" *(see
Matt. 16:26–27; Mark 8:36).*

» I've come to see that Christ is the only way, the only truth, and the only life *(see John 14:6; 17:3; 18:37; 1 John 5:20; CCC 459, 1698)*.

» I know that salvation is through Christ; we can't earn it or buy it *(see Acts 4:12; Rom. 10:9–13; CCC 432, 452)*.

» I believe that Christ died for all of us, so that every single one of us has access to this winning crown *(see John 3:16; James 1:12; Rev. 21:2–4; CCC 219, 458)*.

MY REFLECTIONS

COMMIT TO THESE PRAYERS AND PROMISES

MY NEXT STEP in striving to become holy was to establish a prayer journal, which consists of prayers, meditations, reflections, and Scripture passages through which I felt the Lord was touching my heart. Often, I refer back to these writings in my journal, as the Spirit moves me.

Below are some of the key prayers and promises that have become the foundation of my prayer life. All these are all based on Sacred Scripture, holy meditations, and the teachings of the Church. You may want to use some of these for your own prayers and reflections as you begin your prayer journal.

The Apostles' Creed

The Apostles' Creed is the statement of our belief as Catholics. It was not written by the Apostles but was inspired by their teachings and contains the fundamentals of Christianity in twelve articles. We all need to know and understand it.

» It is recited at Sunday Masses.

» It is prayed at every Baptism.

» It is part of the Rosary and the Divine Mercy Chaplet.

» The twelve articles represent the Twelve Apostles.

» The Creed is thoroughly explained in the **Catechism of the Catholic Church**.

"I believe" (Apostles' Creed) is the faith of the Church professed personally by each believer, principally during Baptism.... "I believe" is also the Church, our mother, responding to God by faith as she teaches us to say both "I believe" and "We believe." (CCC 167)

"The Apostles' Creed is so called because it is rightly considered to be a faithful summary of the Apostles' faith. It is the ancient baptismal symbol of the Church of Rome. Its great authority arises from this fact: it is 'the Creed of the Roman Church, the See of Peter, the first of the apostles, to which he brought the common faith.'" (CCC 194, *quoting St. Ambrose, Expl. symb. 1*)

"As on the day of our Baptism, when our whole life was entrusted to the 'standard of teaching,' let us embrace the Creed of our life-giving faith. To say the Credo with faith is to enter into communion with

God, Father, Son, and Holy Spirit, and also with the whole Church which transmits the faith to us and in whose midst we believe." *(CCC 197)*

"This Creed is the spiritual seal, our heart's meditation and ever-present guardian; it is, unquestionably, the treasure of our souls." *(St. Ambrose)*

MY REFLECTIONS

THE APOSTLES' CREED

I believe in God the Father Almighty,
creator of Heaven and Earth (CCC 199)
and in Jesus Christ, His only Son,
Our Lord (CCC 430),
who was conceived by the Holy Spirit,
born of the Virgin Mary (CCC 456),
suffered under Pontius Pilate, was crucified,
died, and was buried (CCC 571).
He descended into Hell; on the third day
he rose again from the dead (CCC 631).
He ascended into Heaven and is seated at
the right hand of the Father (CCC 659).
From thence He will come again to judge
the living and the dead (CCC 668).
I believe in the Holy Spirit (CCC 683),
the Holy Catholic Church (CCC 748),
the communion of saints (CCC 946),
the forgiveness of sins (CCC 976),
the resurrection of the body (CCC 988),
and life everlasting (CCC 1020).
Amen (CCC 1061).

Say these prayers

Prayers of Faith

My Lord, I believe in You. May I never doubt You. *(John 3:16; 14:1; 20:30–31; Mark 16:16; Phil. 3:7–11; CCC 151)*

My Lord, I love You more than anything else, and I know You love me. *(Rom. 8:31–39; John 14:23; Deut. 6:4–5; CCC 260)*

My Lord, I hope in You, and that hope is the anchor that keeps me grounded in You. *(Rom. 15:13; 1 Pet. 1:3; 1 John 3:3; Rom. 8:24–25; Heb. 6:19–20; CCC 1820, 654)*

Prayers to the Holy Spirit

Holy Spirit, enlighten my mind with thoughts of God, so that I can think and act in ways that please You. *(Isa. 55:8–9; 1 Cor. 2:10–13; Col. 3:2; Eph.1:18; CCC 1003)*

Holy Spirit, inflame my heart with love of God, so that I can love and treat others the way I would like to be treated. *(Matt. 22:36–39; John 13:35; 15:12–14; 1 Cor. 13; CCC 782)*

Holy Spirit, empower me with the energy of Your graces, so that I can handle with courage all challenges and obstacles I face. (*John 14:12; 14:26; 15:5; 1 Pet. 5:8–11; Eph. 1:19*)

Prayers in Confidence

My Lord, I trust in You, for I am certain that You will never abandon me. (*Prov. 3:5–6; Sir. 2:6, 8; Luke 5:1–11; Ps. 31:14; CCC 215*)

My Lord, I long for You, for You are my beginning and end. (*Ps. 84:2; Rev. 1:8; 22:13; CCC 198*)

My Lord, I seek You, for You will lead me on the path to eternal salvation. (*Gal. 1:10; Ps. 105:3–4; 119:10; Isa. 55:6; Deut. 4:29; Matt. 6:33; 7:7–8; CCC 1942*)

Prayers of Adoration

My Lord, I worship You as my Lord and Savior. (*1 Tim. 2:3–5; John 4:23–26; Rev. 5:13–14; 7:9–12; CCC 1179*)

My Lord, I praise You as Father, Son, and Holy Spirit. (*Ps. 104:33–34; 113:1–4; 117; Rev. 19:5–6; CCC 1137, 2639*)

My Lord, I adore You as my Creator and the one true God. *(Ps. 33:13–15; 139; 1 Cor. 8:6; Dan. 2:20–23; CCC 258)*

Prayers of Repentance

My Lord, I call for You, for I know that You are the only sure and safe place to turn. *(Jer. 29:12; Rom. 10:12–13; 11:29, 33–36; Isa. 58:9; Ps. 116:1–2, 4; 145:18; CCC 2666)*

My Lord, I ask forgiveness for my sins, for I know that I am weak and will stumble along the way. *(Rom. 7:15, 19–20; Ps. 32:5; 51:1–2; Matt. 6:14–15; CCC 2838)*

My Lord, I am sorry for my sins, for I know that You are a merciful and loving God. *(Ps. 86:2–5; Titus 3:4–8; Ezek. 18:21–22; Isa. 54:8, 10; CCC 1999)*

MY REFLECTIONS

What these short prayers have taught me

Here is what I finally concluded from many years of meditating on these short prayers.

MY BELIEF IN GOD HAS STRENGTHENED.

The Lord has built up my confidence in Him, so that I never doubt that He is at my side through thick and thin.

MY LOVE FOR HIM HAS GROWN.

My love for the Lord has grown over the years as I have seen how His hand has been on me every step of the way. Now I am confident that God truly loves me unconditionally.

MY HOPE IS MORE ENDURING.

I have learned through too many experiences that putting my hope in myself and other persons leads to many disappointments. When I have put my hope in the Lord, He has never let me down.

MY MIND IS LESS RESTLESS.

Allowing my thoughts to roam has too often led me into temptation and even into sin. Now, when I start losing control of my thoughts and begin heading down the wrong path, I turn to the Holy Spirit and our Blessed Mother for help: they quickly set me back on the right path.

MY HEART IS MORE ROOTED IN GOD.

I've found that the Holy Spirit is the source of love for my heart, and love is the key to all our relationships in this life.

MY LIFE IS CONSCIOUSLY IN GOD'S HANDS.

I've come to see that God knows what's best for me, and He will supply me with the necessary graces to cope with courage in any situation that comes up during my lifetime.

MY TRUST IN HIM HAS MATURED.

I've developed so much trust in the Lord over the years, through the many situations that I have experienced, that I know He will never leave me stranded.

MY REFLECTIONS

I'VE LEARNED TO PERSEVERE.

As I've traveled down this long journey of life, I've come to see through the Word of God and the teaching of the Catholic Church that God is with me, from start to finish.

I REALIZE I MUST SEEK HIM.

I know that as long as I stay focused on God, He will lead me to eternal salvation.

I'VE FOUND PEACE BY WORSHIPING HIM.

When I worshiped the things of this world, I was never truly satisfied. Once I turned to the Lord with all my heart and soul, I found true serenity.

I PRAISE GOD.

Once I realized that the Trinity loves me and cares for me personally, I gave the Trinity all praise and glory.

I ADORE GOD.

After reflecting on my existence and the birth of my children and grandchildren, plus all the other living creatures on the face of the earth, how can I not bow down and adore my Creator and God?

I SEEK FORGIVENESS.

I am a sinner. I fall multiple times. But like Jesus, who fell three times on His way to Calvary and got up each time, I, too, have to get up after I've fallen into sin. I've learned that I just have to go to Confession, start fresh again, and never give up!

I STRIVE TO BE SORRY FOR MY SINS.

I've struggled to awaken in my soul genuine repentance for my sins and then to confess them. When we do this, Jesus can't wait to pour out His mercy on us.

MY REFLECTIONS

Make these promises

The following are action items I have committed to as a result of my prayers and meditations along this pilgrimage and that you should commit to as well.

PROMISE TO YIELD CONTROL

ABANDON **yourself to Divine Providence.**

Realize that God is in control of everything that happens in your life.

Even though I firmly believe that God is totally in charge, I still have occasions in which I try to take control. You can imagine what happens then!

TO READ

- Sir. 39:16, 18
- CCC 302–304
- John 16:13
- CCC 687

LIVE **in the present moment.**

Don't worry about the past or be concerned about the future; concentrate on the present moment.

At times I beat myself up for the things I did in the past, or I begin wondering what's in store

TO READ

- Prov. 19:21
- James 4:13–15
- Isa. 54:7–8
- CCC 307–308

for me and my family in the future. What a waste of time! All we have is the here and now: the present moment.

PROMISE TO BE COURAGEOUS

COMMIT **yourself to the ways of the Lord.**

Don't rely on your ways and ideas; stay focused on God's way.

TO READ

- Ps. 25:1, 4, 8–10
- Sir. 3:20–24
- Prov. 4:10–13
- CCC 1731–1732

I spent a large part of my life living according to my ways, not God's ways. Well, hell is filled with my ways! Now I pray daily and ask God to show me the way.

PERSEVERE **through all obstacles.**

Whether you are in a trial, about to face one, or have just passed through one, ask the Holy Spirit for the strength to persevere.

TO READ

- Matt. 10:22
- Heb. 12:1–2;
- Rom. 8:38–39
- 1 Cor. 10:13
- CCC 1821

I have experienced many trials and tribulations that have caused me anxiety and heartache. Much of the anxiety was brought on by my asking God, "Why me?" We won't get an answer to that question until we reach heaven. These days, this is my prayer: "Lord, I accept whatever You give me, but please give me the strength to deal with it." He supplies me with the necessary graces.

PROMISE TO OBEY GOD

ABIDE **by the Word of the Lord.**

First, listen for the Word of the
Lord. Then obey it.

TO READ

- Acts 5:28–32
- John 13:12–15
- Isa. 1:18–20
- CCC 450

I know very well that it's one
thing to read the Word of God and
another to put it into action. I've
learned that I need to meditate
on the Word and then listen to the Lord speak to my heart.
He gives us what we need, not what we want—if we only obey.

DISCIPLINE **your body, mind, and spirit.**

Each day, take control of your
thoughts, take care of your body,
and rely on the Holy Spirit.

TO READ

- Rom. 12:1–2
- Heb. 12:5–11
- Wisd. 3:5
- CCC 270, 1709

Once, I realized that my body
is a temple of the Holy Spirit, it
changed my whole perspective
on life. Our lives must be balanced—spiritually, mentally,
and physically.

PROMISE TO SUBMIT TO HIS WILL

HUMBLE yourself before the Lord.

Continually remind yourself that you can accomplish nothing without God's help.

TO READ

- 1 Pet. 5:6
- Matt. 19:26
- Luke 14:11; 18:14
- CCC 308

Pride and ego created great roadblocks to my spiritual growth. Humility taught me to serve others rather than take care of my self-interests.

BE PATIENT

What do you gain by becoming impatient or anxious? It only makes things worse!

TO READ

- James 5:7–8
- Matt. 6:33–34
- Rom. 2:6–8
- CCC 2830, 2547

This is one area of I need to work on constantly; I really struggle against impatience. It gives me grief! I have made good progress over the years, but I must continually ask the Holy Spirit to help me to become a more patient person.

PROMISE TO SEEK CONTENTMENT

BE ALERT, **for you do not know the hour of your death.**

Remember: only one person knows the time and the place—and He's not passing out the information. So just relax and be prepared at all times.

TO READ

- Matt. 24:42–44; 25:13
- Mark 13:32–33, 37
- John 16:33
- CCC 673

When I was younger, I never really thought much about death, but as I grew up, I started thinking to myself, "If I faced death, what would my reaction be—sad, glad, or mad?" Well, I did face death! I found out that I was not fearful of death. I didn't want to go, but I knew that I was prepared and at peace because I had been living as a "godly man" for many years.

BE JOYFUL **in the Lord.**

It will bring you true peace and happiness.

TO READ

- Rom. 14:17–19
- John 16:22, 24
- Isa. 35:10
- Luke 2:10
- CCC 2819

For many years, I was looking for joy, peace, and happiness in all the wrong places. When I made the Lord my number-one priority, I found true joy, peace, and happiness—as much as we can on this earth.

SERVE the Lord faithfully.

He has done great things for you.

The closer I grew to the Lord, the more I wanted to know Him, to love Him, and to serve Him.

TO READ

- Luke 4:8
- John 12:26
- 1 Sam. 12:24
- Mark 9:35
- Sir. 2:1
- Rom. 14:18
- Josh. 24:14, 15, 18, 24
- CCC 2084, 2096

MY REFLECTIONS

LIVE BY THESE GODLY LIFE PRINCIPLES

ONCE I HAD ESTABLISHED God's Winning Formula in my heart and developed a solid prayer life, I began to formulate a list of godly life principles to be the standard that I would try to live by.

My personal goals and objectives are all based on these godly principles. These aren't just words on a piece of paper but the way that I try to live each day.

These principles were formulated over an extended period of time. Their content comes from multiple sources: Scripture, the *Catechism*, prayer, meditation, and my own experiences (which include many ups and downs).

I suggest that you review and reflect on these godly principles, in hopes that they may encourage you to establish your own set of principles.

Love God with your whole heart, soul, and mind.

(Matt. 22:37; Rom. 8:38–39; Deut. 6:4–6; CCC 201, 2083–84)

» Carry out His will always as your highest priority. He always looks out for your best interests.

» Continue to build a closer personal relationship with the Lord. He will be there for you at all times.

» Radiate the light of Christ. It's the only way to overcome darkness.

» Pray often with intense focus on faith. Prayer is conversation with God from the bottom of your heart.

MY REFLECTIONS

_____

_____

_____

_____

_____

_____

_____

_____

_____

_____

Love one another.

(Matt. 22:39; Gal. 5:14; John 15:17; CCC 2055, 2067, 2069)

» Love your wife first, then your children, and then the rest of your family. (You have a covenant with your wife. Eventually, your children will leave to start their own lives.)

» Love your friends especially, and the people you work with. Loyal friends are hard to come by—cherish them.

» Make no judgment about others without having all the facts. You don't know what's going on in their lives.

» Help those around you to feel important. Build people up; don't tear them down.

» Serve the largest number of people you can, in the most effective way. You will receive much more gratification in serving others than you will in serving yourself.

MY REFLECTIONS

Love yourself.

(1 Cor. 6:19–20; Gal. 2:20; 1 John 4:16; CCC 478, 27)

» Don't bruise your self-esteem. Don't think less of yourself; think of yourself less.
» Develop a sense of personal worth. After all, you are made in the image and likeness of God.
» Maintain a positive attitude toward yourself. Negative attitudes will drag you down.
» Always remember that God loves you—unconditionally!

MY REFLECTIONS

_____

_____

_____

_____

_____

_____

_____

_____

_____

Have faith in God, in yourself, and in others.

(1 John 5:4–5; 1 Tim. 6:11–12; CCC 150–155)

» Have complete loyalty to God's will. Abandon yourself to Divine Providence. God created each of us, and He has a plan for our lives.

» Have confidence in yourself but remember that you can accomplish nothing without God.

» Have confidence in friends, and the people you work with. True friends will be with you through thick and thin.

» Have respect for the dignity of all human beings from conception to natural death.

MY REFLECTIONS

Be spiritually self-reliant.

(Prov. 3:5–6; Isa. 55:8–9; CCC 1709, 1711)

» Hold fast to your convictions when you know in your heart that you are right. Make sure these convictions are from God.

» Do right even when others are doing wrong. Don't fall for the excuse "Everyone else is doing it."

» Listen to the Lord and not to the persuasions of man. Proper discernment is the key *(Isa. 55:3)*.

» Be a man of integrity! Your word is your bond.

MY REFLECTIONS

_____

_____

_____

_____

_____

_____

_____

_____

_____

Be humble.

(Luke 18:14; James 4:10; 2 Cor. 3:5; CCC 308)

» Free yourself from boasting, arrogance, egotism, and self-centeredness. Everything that you possess is a gift from God.

» Be teachable. Don't act like a know-it-all.

» Know yourself as you really are. Don't put on an act. Be yourself.

» Seek not the plaudits of others. The only one we need to please is God. Our power comes from one source: the Holy Spirit.

MY REFLECTIONS

Be an outstanding husband, father, grandfather.

(Prov. 4:20–23; Eph. 6:4; CCC 2215–2230)

» Build strong family unity. Honor God first, and then your family *(Sir. 3:1–6)*.
» Spend meaningful time with your wife and family. Don't just be physically present: give them your full attention.
» Help them with spiritual, intellectual, social, professional, physical, and financial needs. Help them grow by sharing your past experiences.
» Commit them to the Lord by lifting them up in prayer and placing them under the protection of the Blessed Virgin Mary. "As for me and my house, we will serve the Lord" *(Josh. 24:15)*.

MY REFLECTIONS

Be honest in all your thoughts, feelings, and deeds.

(John 1:4–5; Ps. 24:3–5; CCC 1216)

» Have nothing to do with hypocrisy. Don't be a phony!

» Be very open, with no part of you in darkness. Be transparent at all times.

» Make sure that you are fair and completely above board. Don't play favorites! Treat everyone with respect.

» See that justice is properly administered. Be fair and honest in all matters. No partiality!

MY REFLECTIONS

Strive never to be angry with others.

(Prov. 14:17; 15:1, 18; James 1:19–21; CCC 1765, 2262)

» Nurture an even temperament. Do more listening than giving opinions.
» Be patient and long-suffering with all people and situations. You can disagree with somebody without "blowing your stack."
» Develop a gentle spirit. You will accomplish much by staying on an even keel.

MY REFLECTIONS

Nurture a charismatic personality.

(Phil. 4:4–7; Gal. 5:22; CCC 735–736, 1880)

» Wear a radiant smile. A nice smile will knock down many barriers.
» Develop a spontaneous sense of humor. Don't take yourself too seriously. Chill out!
» Maintain high level of alertness. Stay on top of things.
» Project a positive attitude. There is enough negativity; people are fed up with it!

MY REFLECTIONS

Use refined speech.

(James 3:5–10; Matt. 5:33, 37; CCC 2464, 2466, 2475)

» Avoid all forms of profanity and vulgar language. We need to build up, not tear down.

» Speak directly, with simple, concise words. Let your "yes" be "yes" and your "no" be "no." Don't beat around the bush.

» Be persuasive and descriptive with your needs. Don't embellish your words to build yourself up.

» Watch your tongue. It can either be a destructive device or a loving tool.

MY REFLECTIONS

_____

_____

_____

_____

_____

_____

_____

_____

_____

Exercise good judgment.

(Matt. 7:1–4; CCC 2477–78)

» Base your decisions on facts, objective reasoning, life principles, and the Lord's inspiration. Be sure that proper discernment plays a major role in your decision-making process.

» Before making decisions, pray to the Holy Spirit. In most major decisions, the answer comes from the heart.

» Avoid all forms of judgmentalism. Who are we to judge others? We don't know what others are going through *(James 4:12)*.

MY REFLECTIONS

Be a leader (in the true sense of the word).

(Heb. 13:7; CCC 899–901)

» Be of good character. Face the trials and tribulations of this life courageously.

» Show the right way by going first. Why would someone follow you if you haven't gone first?

» Demonstrate the best method of achieving goals, and tackle them with commitment, endurance, and confidence.

» Lead by example and action, not by words.

MY REFLECTIONS

_____

_____

_____

_____

_____

_____

_____

_____

_____

Use material goods for spiritual ends.

(Luke 12:20–21; Matt. 6:19–21, 24; CCC 2407, 2551, 2556)

» Your wealth is to be used to further God's kingdom. You can't take it with you!

» Remember that possessions are a gift from God rather than things you earned. You will be held accountable for the way you use them.

» Practice tithing to the Church. You can't outgive the Lord. You can't serve two masters.

> "For what does it profit a man, to gain the whole world and forfeit his soul?" *(Sir. 35:8–11; Matt. 6:3–4; Mark 8:36).*

MY REFLECTIONS

CREATE YOUR OWN PERSONAL SPIRITUAL WORKOUT PLAN

AS I JOURNEYED down the road toward holiness, I came to realize that to remain faithful for this long trip, I must be committed to a personal Spiritual Workout Plan and also join with others on the same journey.

To date, my personal Spiritual Workout Plan and my involvement in small spiritual-accountability groups have kept me on course, despite many obstacles along the way. Without such a plan, there is no way that I would have made it over these thirty-five years. Your plan should have four cornerstones.

PRAYER   THE LITURGY

EUCHARISTIC
ADORATION   CONFESSION

1. Prayer

*(Luke 18:1; 11:1–4, 9; Phil. 4:6–8; 1
Tim. 2:1–4; CCC 2558–2865)*

WHAT PRAYER IS

Christian prayer is a covenant relationship between God and man in Christ. It is the action of God and of man, springing forth from both the Holy Spirit and ourselves, wholly directed to the Father, in union with the human will of the Son of God made man. *(CCC 2564)*

In the New Covenant, prayer is the living relationship of the children of God with their Father who is good beyond measure, with his Son Jesus Christ and with the Holy Spirit. *(CCC 2565)*

WE SHOULD PRAY ALONG WITH OUR READING OF THE SCRIPTURES

The Church "forcefully and specially exhorts all the Christian faithful … to learn 'the surpassing knowledge of Jesus Christ' *(Phil. 3:8)* by frequent reading of the divine Scriptures.... Let them remember, however, that prayer should accompany the reading of Sacred Scripture, so that a dialogue takes place between God and man. For 'we speak to him when we pray; we listen to him when we read divine oracles.'" *(CCC 2653)*

THE FORMS OF PRAYER (*CCC 2626–2643*)

- **Blessing:** God blesses us and we bless Him in return for His blessing.

- **Adoration:** We acknowledge the greatness and power of God.

- **Petition:** We cry out to God with our needs.

- **Intercession:** We petition God on behalf of others.

- **Thanksgiving:** We thank God for the many blessings He has showered on us and on others, and even for the fact that He is God.

MY REFLECTIONS

_____

_____

_____

_____

_____

_____

_____

_____

2. The liturgy

(John 6:53–55; Luke 22:19; 1 Cor. 10:16–17; CCC 1322–1419)

The Eucharist is "the source and summit of the Christian life." *(CCC 1324; LG 11)*

The liturgy of the Word and the liturgy of the Eucharist together form "one single act of worship"; the Eucharistic table set for us is the table both of the Word of God and the Body of the Lord. *(CCC 1346; SC 56; DV 21)*

1 Cor. 11:23–26 tells us and the Church teaches us that Jesus Christ came to earth, suffered, died, was buried, rose from the dead, and ascended into heaven. He instituted the sacrament of Holy Eucharist at the Last Supper, offering us His true and Real Presence in His Body, Blood, Soul, and Divinity. If we truly believe that, why wouldn't we want to receive the Eucharist as often as possible?

MY REFLECTIONS

---

3. Eucharistic adoration

(Rev. 7:9–11; Ps. 95:6; CCC 1378–1379)

Many churches have periods of adoration in which a consecrated Host is displayed in a monstrance. Some churches have chapels for perpetual adoration, which is prayer before a Host that is exposed continuously. The Forty Hours devotion is practiced in many churches that do not have perpetual adoration.

Many answers to major decisions in my life came while I was in Eucharistic adoration. The Lord speaks to our hearts while we are quiet and rest in the Spirit.

MY REFLECTIONS

4. Confession

(1 John 1:9–10; 2:2; John 20:21–23; CCC 1455–58)

Sin is before all else an offense against God, a rupture of communion with him. At the same time it damages communion with the Church. For this reason conversion entails both God's forgiveness and reconciliation with the Church, which are expressed and accomplished liturgically by the sacrament of Penance and Reconciliation. *(CCC 1440; LG 11)*

The spiritual effects of Confession are recovery of graces, peace and serenity of conscience, spiritual consolation, and spiritual strength for the Christian battle.

How can I repay the Lord, for all He has done for me?

I decided that the best way that I could thank Him is with my own Spiritual Workout.

MY REFLECTIONS

MY OWN SPIRITUAL WORKOUT
(Should you make it yours?)

Regular prayers
Daily, I pray early in the morning, and that time includes reading Scripture and meditating on it. In the evening, my wife and I have a shorter prayer time, focusing on various topics. I pray the Rosary and the Divine Mercy Chaplet each day (usually during my exercise workout).

Daily Mass
Each day my wife and I attend Mass. It's the most important part of our day. If we miss it for whatever reason, it leaves a void.

Monthly Eucharistic adoration
At least once a month, but when the Spirit moves us, my wife and I spend time in Eucharistic adoration. We have resolved to go more in the New Year.

Monthly Confession
My wife and I go to Confession once a month. My wife says I should go more often! Note: we have built up to

(continued)

MY OWN SPIRITUAL WORKOUT (*CONTINUED*)

this over the years. Also, we are seniors and have more time. (Whether or not you are retired, now is the time to start your own Spiritual Workout or build upon the one you already have.)

Small accountability groups with communal prayer and sharing (*Luke 6:12–13; 10:1–2; Eph. 2:19–22; Matt. 18:20*)

> Iron sharpens iron, and one man sharpens another. (*Prov. 27:17*)

> Two are better than one, because they have a good reward for their toil. For if they fall, one will lift up his fellow; but woe to him who is alone when he falls and has not another to lift him up. And though a man might prevail against one who is alone, two will withstand him. A threefold cord is not quickly broken. (*Eccles. 4:9–10, 12*)

Jesus formed the first small accountability group among the Apostles. They were just ordinary guys like you and me. Jesus taught and trained them and sent them out by twos to spread the gospel and start new groups. We can do the same.

Our Monday night disciples group (*CCC 2689*)
Started at my house over thirty years ago, this group still meets weekly and has spawned other groups in the New Orleans area. Some have formed outreach programs such as building caskets for indigent babies who have died, prison ministry, and praying on Saturdays at Planned Parenthood facilities.

Our Crossing the Goal ministry
I founded this ministry in 2008 to evangelize men by utilizing small accountability groups and Spiritual Fitness Workouts. Go to our website at www.crossingthegoal.com to learn how to start a group or do an individual workout. Since 1985, I have either started or participated in men's accountability groups because I need to be around my Christian brothers. They can help you, too!

CLOSING PRAYERS

A PRAYER TO LEAD A GODLY LIFE

For the grace of God has appeared for the salvation of all men, training us to renounce irreligion and worldly passions, and to live sober, upright, and godly lives in this world, awaiting our blessed hope, the appearing of the glory of our great God and Savior Jesus Christ, who gave himself for us to redeem us from all iniquity and to purify for himself a people of his own who are zealous for good deeds. *(Titus 2:11–14)*

A PRAYER FOR INTERIOR PEACE

Peace I leave with you; my peace I give to you; not as the world gives do I give to you. Let not your hearts be troubled, neither let them be afraid. *(John 14:27)*

But now in Christ Jesus you who once were far off have been brought near in the blood of Christ. For he is our peace, who has made us both one, and has broken down the dividing wall of hostility, by abolishing in his flesh the law of commandments and ordinances, that he might create in himself one new man in place of the two, so making peace, and might reconcile us both to God in one body through the cross, thereby bringing the hostility to an end. And he came and preached peace to you who were far off and peace to those who were near; for through him we both have access in one Spirit to the Father. *(Eph. 2:13–18)*

Earthly peace is the image and fruit of the peace of Christ, the messianic "Prince of Peace." By the blood of his Cross, "in his own person he killed the hostility," he reconciled men with God and made his Church the sacrament of the unity of the human race and of its union with God. "He is our peace." He has declared: "Blessed are the peacemakers. *(CCC 2305)*

THE PRAYER OF JOHN THE BAPTIST

"He must increase, but I must decrease." *(John 3:30)*

THE PRAYER OF OUR BLESSED MOTHER

"Do whatever He tells you." *(John 2:5)*

Sophia Institute

Sophia Institute is a nonprofit institution that seeks to nurture the spiritual, moral, and cultural life of souls and to spread the Gospel of Christ in conformity with the authentic teachings of the Roman Catholic Church.

Sophia Institute Press fulfills this mission by offering translations, reprints, and new publications that afford readers a rich source of the enduring wisdom of mankind.

Sophia Institute also operates the popular online resource CatholicExchange.com. *Catholic Exchange* provides world news from a Catholic perspective as well as daily devotionals and articles that will help readers to grow in holiness and live a life consistent with the teachings of the Church.

In 2013, Sophia Institute launched Sophia Institute for Teachers to renew and rebuild Catholic culture through service to Catholic education. With the goal of nurturing the spiritual, moral, and cultural life of souls, and an abiding respect for the role and work of teachers, we strive to provide materials and programs that are at once enlightening to the mind and ennobling to the heart; faithful and complete, as well as useful and practical.

Sophia Institute gratefully recognizes the Solidarity Association for preserving and encouraging the growth of our apostolate over the course of many years. Without their generous and timely support, this book would not be in your hands.

www.SophiaInstitute.com
www.CatholicExchange.com
www.SophiaInstituteforTeachers.org

Sophia Institute Press® is a registered trademark of Sophia Institute.
Sophia Institute is a tax-exempt institution as defined by the
Internal Revenue Code, Section 501(c)(3). Tax ID 22-2548708.